Editor

Eric Migliaccio

Managing Editor

Ina Massler Levin, M.A.

Illustrator

Vicki Frazier

Cover Artist

Barb Lorseyedi

Art Manager

Kevin Barnes

Art Director

CJae Froshay

Imaging

Rosa C. See

Publisher

Mary D. Smith, M.S. Ed.

GRADES K–2

Author

Maria Elvira Gallardo, M.A.

Teacher Created Resources, Inc.

6421 Industry Way

Westminster, CA 92683

www.teachercreated.com

ISBN: 978-1-4206-3126-5

©2005 Teacher Created Resources, Inc.

Reprinted, 2007

Made in U.S.A.

Table of Contents

Introduction

More than ever, it is important for students to practice writing on a daily basis. Every classroom teacher knows that the key to getting students excited about writing is introducing interesting topics that are fun to write about. *September Daily Journal Writing Prompts* provides K–2 teachers with an entire month of ready-to-use journal topics, including special holiday and seasonal topics for September. All journal topics are included in a calendar that is easily reproduced for students. A student journal cover allows students to personalize their journal for the month.

Other useful pages that are fun include:

✣ A Blank Calendar (pages 6 and 7)

This can be used to meet your own classroom needs. You may want your students to come up with their own topics for the month, or it may come in handy for homework writing topics.

✣ Word Banks (pages 40–43)

These include commonly used vocabulary words for school, holiday, and seasonal topics. A blank word bank gives students a place to write other words they have learned throughout the month.

✣ September Author Birthdays (page 44)

Celebrate famous authors' birthdays or introduce an author that is new to your students. This page includes the author's birthdays and titles of some of their most popular books.

✣ September Historic Events (page 45)

In the format of a time line, this page is a great reference tool for students. They will love seeing amazing events that happened in September.

✣ September Discoveries & Inventions (page 46)

Kindle students' curiosity about discoveries and inventions with this page. This is perfect to use for your science and social studies classes.

Motivate your students' writing by reproducing the pages in this book and making each student an individual journal. Use all the journal topics included, or pick and choose them as you please. See the Binding Ideas on page 48 for ways to put it all together. Planning a month of writing will never be easier!

Monthly Calendar

S E P T

1 On the first day of school…	**2** No one but me knows…	**3** When it's rainy weather, I…	**4** My favorite animal is…
9 The best time I ever had was…	**10** Something strange that I have seen is…	**11** The best part of school is…	**12** When I first wake up…
17 I have always wanted to…	**18** My favorite activity is…	**19** I wish my parents…	**20** Having a pet is…
25 I feel so happy when...	**26** Homework is…	**27** What I like the most about myself is…	**28** When I'm bored…

September Daily Journal Writing Prompts

Monthly Calendar (cont.)

EMBER

5
On weekends I like to…

6
I was really embarrassed when…

7
After school I always…

8
I always laugh when…

13
Playing games is fun because…

14
My best friend is…

15
It makes me tired when…

16
When I grow up, I want to be…

21
I love reading…

22
If I had three wishes…

23
I want to learn all about…

24
What really drives me crazy is…

29
If only my teacher…

30
I would love to visit…

Special Topics

Labor Day
A good job is important because…

Autumn
My favorite part of autumn…

Blank Monthly Calendar

S	E	P	T
1	2	3	4
9	10	11	12
17	18	19	20
25	26	27	28

Blank Monthly Calendar *(cont.)*

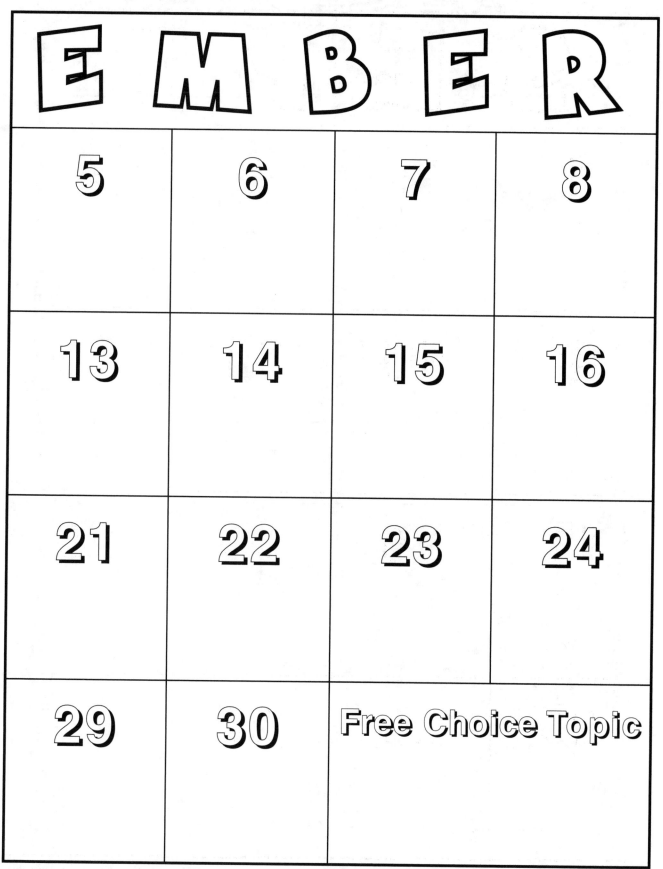

EMBER			
5	6	7	8
13	14	15	16
21	22	23	24
29	30	Free Choice Topic	

On the first day of school _____

_____

_____

_____

_____

_____

_____

_____

_____

    8

No one but me knows _____

_____

_____

_____

_____

_____

_____

_____

When it's rainy weather, I _____

_____

_____

_____

_____

_____

_____

_____

_____

My favorite animal is _____

_____

_____

_____

_____

_____

_____

_____

On weekends I like to _____

_____

_____

_____

_____

_____

_____

_____

I was really embarassed when _____

_____

_____

_____

_____

_____

_____

_____

_____

After school I always _____

_____

_____

_____

_____

_____

_____

_____

_____

I always laugh when _____

_____

_____

_____

_____

_____

_____

_____

The best time I ever had was _____

_____

_____

_____

_____

_____

_____

_____

Something strange that I have seen is _____

_____

_____

_____

_____

_____

_____

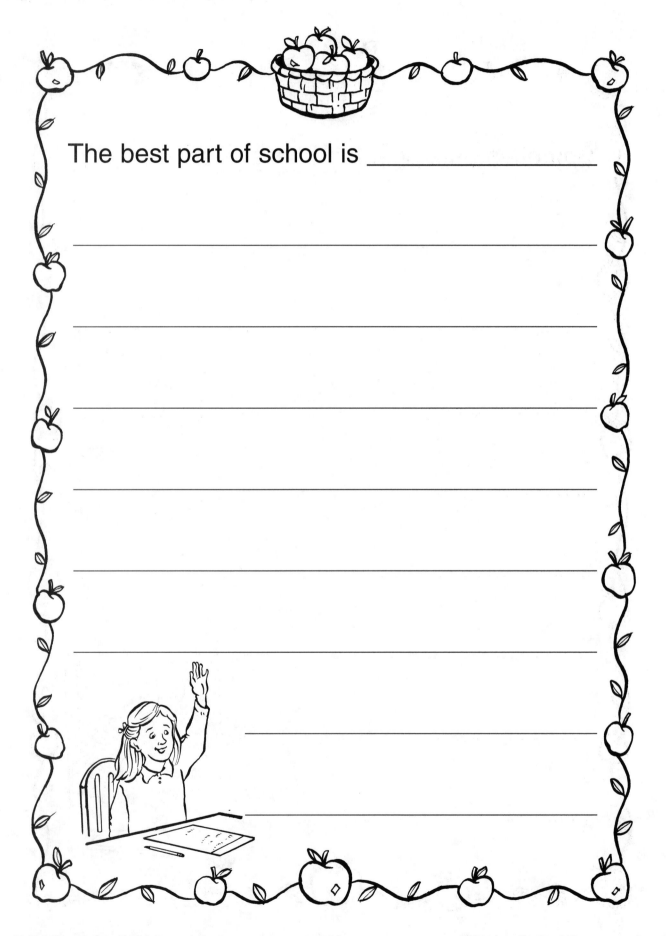

The best part of school is _____

_____

_____

_____

_____

_____

_____

_____

When I first wake up _____

_____

_____

_____

_____

_____

_____

_____

Playing games is fun because _____

_____

_____

_____

_____

_____

_____

_____

_____

My best friend is _____

_____

_____

_____

_____

_____

_____

_____

_____

It makes me tired when _____

_____

_____

_____

_____

_____

_____

When I grow up, I want to be _____

_____

_____

_____

_____

_____

_____

_____

I have always wanted to _____

_____

_____

_____

_____

_____

_____

_____

_____

My favorite activity is _____

_____

_____

_____

_____

_____

_____

_____

I wish my parents _____

_____

_____

_____

_____

_____

_____

_____

26

Having a pet is _____

_____

_____

_____

_____

_____

_____

_____

_____

I love reading _____

_____

_____

_____

_____

_____

_____

_____

If I had three wishes _____

_____

_____

_____

_____

_____

_____

_____

I want to learn all about _____

_____

_____

_____

_____

_____

_____

_____

30

What really drives me crazy is _____

_____

_____

_____

_____

_____

_____

_____

_____

I feel so happy when _____

_____

_____

_____

_____

_____

_____

_____

Homework is _____

_____

_____

_____

_____

_____

_____

_____

_____

What I like the most about myself is _____

When I'm bored _____

_____

_____

_____

_____

_____

_____

_____

If only my teacher _____

_____

_____

_____

_____

_____

_____

$33 + 22 =$ _____

_____

I would love to visit _____

_____

_____

_____

_____

_____

_____

_____

A good job is important because _____

_____

_____

_____

_____

_____

_____

_____

_____

38

My favorite part of autumn is _____

_____

_____

_____

_____

_____

_____

_____

_____

School Word Bank

activity	desks	map	recess
art	dictionary	markers	report
assembly	flag	math	ruler
award	games	music	science
backpack	glue	office	scissors
board	grades	paper	spelling
books	history	pencils	students
calendar	homework	pens	subject
classroom	learn	playground	teacher
computer	library	principal	test
crayons	lunch	reading	write

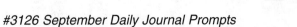

Holiday Word Bank

September Holidays

American Indian Day

Labor Day

Rosh Hashanah (Jewish New Year, Day of Remembrance)

Yom Kippur (Jewish Day of Atonement)

Grandparents' Day

Mexican Independence Day

career	government	relatives
caring	grandma	religious
celebrate	grandpa	revolution
challah	holy	shofar
culture	honor	special
customs	job	symbols
education	kin	synagogue
family	loving	traditions
festival	parade	tribes
forgiveness	prayers	workers

Seasonal Word Bank

	fall	pumpkin
	foliage	rake
	frost	red
	geese	scarecrow
acorn	harvest	September
apple	hay	squash
autumn	jacket	squirrel
breeze	leaves	trees
brown	maple	wind
chestnut	November	yellow
chilly	October	
cider	orange	
colorful	pear	
cool		

My Word Bank

September Author Birthdays

3

Aliki

(b. 1929)

A Medieval Feast (1983, Ty Crowell Co.)

Feelings (1984, Harper Collins)

8

Jon Scieszka

(b. 1954)

The Stinky Cheese Man (1992, Viking)

The True Story of the Three Little Pigs! (1996, Puffin)

13

Roald Dahl

(1916–1990)

James and the Giant Peach (1961, Knopf)

Charlie and the Chocolate Factory (1964, Knopf)

15

Tomie DePaola

(b. 1934)

26 Fairmont Avenue (1999, Putnam)

Here We All Are (2000, Putnam)

16

H.A. Rey

(1898–1977)

Curious George (1941, Houghton Mifflin)

Curious George Gets a Medal (1957, Houghton Mifflin)

18

Joanne Ryder

(b. 1946)

The Snail's Spell (1998, Puffins)

Earthdance (1999, Henry Holt)

Come Along, Kitten (2003, Simon & Schuster)

21

Taro Yashima

(b. 1908)

Crow Boy (1955, Viking Press)

Momo's Kitten (1961, Viking Press)

22

Olivier Dunrea

(b. 1953)

Bear Noel (2000, Farrar Straus & Giroux)

It's Snowing! (2002, Farrar Straus & Giroux)

25

Shel Silverstein

(1930–1999)

The Giving Tree (1964, Harper & Row)

Where the Sidewalk Ends (1974, Harper & Row)

A Light in the Attic (1981, Harper & Row)

27

Bernard Waber

(b. 1924)

Lyle, Lyle, Crocodile (1973, Walter Lorraine Books)

Loveable Lyle (1977, Walter Lorraine Books)

29

Marissa Moss

(b. 1959)

Amelia's Notebook (1995, Ten Speed Press)

Amelia Writes Again (1999, Pleasant Company)

29

Stan Berenstain

(b. 1924)

The Berenstain Bears' New Baby (1974, Random House)

The Berenstain Bears Go to School (1978, Random House)

September Historic Events

September 4, 1781

The city of Los Angeles was founded in southwest California.

September 5, 1882

The first labor day parade was held in New York City.

September 7, 1909

The first junior high school was opened in Columbus, Ohio.

September 9, 1850

California became the 31st state of the United States.

September 12, 1959

Luna 2, the first spacecraft to land on the moon, was launched by the USSR.

September 16, 1620

The *Mayflower* left Plymouth, England and landed in what is now Massachusetts two months later.

September 17, 1787

The Constitution was approved and signed in Pennsylvania.

September 19, 1928

Walt Disney debuted Mickey Mouse in a cartoon called *Steamboat Willie.*

September 20, 1519

Magellan led the first expedition to travel completely around the globe.

September 22, 1862

Abraham Lincoln freed the slaves in the Emancipation Proclamation.

September 24, 1957

For the first time, African-American and white students attended the same school in Little Rock, Arkansas.

September Discoveries & Inventions

4

The first electric lighting by Thomas Edison in 1882. Four hundred electric lights lit up offices in lower Manhattan, New York.

Kodak camera patented by George Eastman in 1888. He further invented photographic film and paper that enable people to take photographs.

12 **Prehistoric paintings** were discovered in 1940 by five boys playing in a cave in southwestern France.

18 **Crayola Crayons** were created for kids in 1903 by Edwin Binney and C. Harold Smith in Pennsylvania.

21

Bubble gum was invented in 1928 by Walter Diemer. He called his invention "Dubble Bubble."

Velcro was created in 1955 by George de Mestral in Switzerland.

22 **It's the ice-cream cone's birthday**. It was invented in 1903 by Italo Marchiony.

21

The planet Neptune was seen for the first time by German astronomers J.C. Galle and H.d' Arrest in 1846.

The Pacific Ocean was discovered in 1513 by Vasco Nunez de Balboa, a Spanish conquistador.

25 **The zipper gets its name** by B.F. Goodrich in 1923. It was previously called the "separable fastener" and "clasp locker."

28 **Discovery of California** in 1542 by Portuguese navigator Juan Rodriguez Cabrillo, who reached San Diego Bay.

30 **The patent for the stapler** was granted to Samuel Slocum in 1841. He called it a machine "for sticking pins into paper."

September Journal

by

_____

Binding Ideas

Students will be so delighted when they see a month of their writing come together with one of the following binding ideas. You may choose to bind their journals at the beginning or end of the month, once they have already filled all of the journal topic pages. When ready to bind students' journals, have them color in their journal cover on page 47. It may be a good idea to reproduce the journal covers on hard stock paper in order to better protect the pages in the journal. Use the same hard stock paper for the back cover.

Simple Book Binding

1. Put all pages in order and staple together along the left margin.

2. Cut book-binding tape to the exact length of the book.

3. Run the center line of tape along the left side of the book and fold to cover the front left margin and the back right margin. Your book is complete!

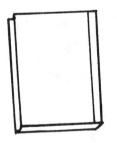

Yarn-Sewn Binding

1. Put all pages in order and hole-punch the left margin.

2. Stitch the pages together with thick yarn or ribbon.